Textures of Spurn

Alice Fox
Spurn Point Artist in Residence 2012

Created to accompany the exhibition *Textures of Spurn*.

Compiled by Alice Fox with support from Nigel Morgan and Ruth Brown.

www.alicefox.co.uk

Printed by Imprint Colour Printers Ltd., Lincoln. www.imprintcolourprinters.com

First published in Great Britain in 2012 by SC Publications, Stone Creek House, Sunk Island, East Yorkshire, HU12 0AP. Email: info@sc-publications.co.uk Tel: 01964 630630

ISBN: 978-0-9554647-2-0

A copy of this publication has been registered with the British Library

Introduction

This book was made to accompany the exhibition *Textures of Spurn*.
It records Alice Fox's six-month residency at Spurn National Nature
Reserve in East Yorkshire during 2012. The residency was based at the
Old Lighthouse, a heritage building that also hosted the residency exhibition
before the work's gallery tour.

The Spurn Artist in Residence program has been run by Yorkshire Wildlife
Trust since 2007. It invites artists to explore the environmental and cultural
processes and histories of a unique landscape. Previous artists have
worked in a variety of media, from sound and found pieces
to formal painting and sculpture.

The residency was documented on a blog:

www.spurnpointartistinresidence.blogspot.co.uk

16.3.12

On the beach I walk west to east round the tip of the point. It's
mainly cloudy with odd breaks in cloud cover letting sunlight
shine on the water. There is a steady, unforgiving wind.

Man-made structures give punctuation to this place: the
utilitarian life boat station with its nest of houses; the left over 'pill
boxes'; the piece-meal road; power lines to the pilots' post; the
finger of the lighthouse; row upon row of groynes – unkempt but
sculptural.

Patterns in the sand seem repetitive and random. Items
are scattered and dropped, sorted and pummelled, dumped
indiscriminately – natural and man-made treated the same.
Water and wind make waves in the sand. These waves are rich
in tiny variations, ever-amplified over time.

Pebbles accumulate in differing densities – some crowd together,
others have space to breathe. The array of colour is surprising,
with nature's subdued tones interrupted by lurid scraps of plastic,
textile, rusty metal, and bits of rope. Within a few metres of each
other I find three gaudy hard hats sitting in the sand.

20.4.12

For two hours I walk a small section of the estuary shore. Rusty objects abound, evidence of the disintegrating defences. I become absorbed in drawing the patterns of the sand.

Above, dramatic grey clouds threaten rain at any time. At eye level a kestrel glides, hunts the marram grass by the lighthouse, working its way north along the dune.

The dusky sage-green leaves of sea buckthorn have appeared. There are bait-diggers on the estuary sand exposed by the retreating tide. Grimsby dock tower is clearly visible across the water.

Now I walk from Warren Cottage, first by the crashing waves on the seaward side, then by the lapping tide on the estuary edge. Walking back again I pick up items for collagraphs and maybe woven pieces

… Could I weave something small each visit?

21.4.12

Grey cold and damp today. There's a steady
drizzle. I walk on the estuary side where the
tide is going down. On this flat shallow side
the tide moves quickly, revealing mud flats and
the strip of salt marsh.

I draw the band of texture where land and
water meet. Birds sit about in groups, flying
every now and then. The visiting birders tell
me there are curlew, godwits, and plovers. I'm
embarrassed by my lack of knowledge.

It starts to rain, lightly, then heavier, then hail!
I'm wet, but decide to keep walking. After
further bouts of hail, the rain stops, though
thunder rolls in the distance. The waves
thunder too. I witness spectacularly large
showers moving across the horizon. Perhaps
I will dry off in the wind before the next shower
reaches me.

9.5.12

At the lighthouse,
and settled into the second floor room,
I draw the waves, my marks made
with a feather and coffee,

A grey windy day,
and by mid afternoon the drizzle clears.
Wind on my back, I wander on the beach.
Waves crashing on my left, I search for rusty metal.
Tiny caterpillars are striking out across the sand.
Where are they going? They look so determined.

I draw more waves. I draw their relentless movement.
One after another after another after another . . .

From the top of the lighthouse
I can see the sideways movement of long-shore drift:
so obvious, so constant this shift of sand and stone.

A fisherman wonders what I'm doing:
I'm wetting fabric in the sea for dyeing.
Tide almost up, each pounding wave
threatens a soaking.

18.5.12

I make a bee-line for the water. Bait diggers' sand piles
litter the beach. I spot the marks of another bait hunter:
a wading bird. Here is a swathe of distinctive marks
made by a long beak systematically thrust into the sand
whilst slowly moving forward. The trail loops and curls.
Suddenly a full stop: a different mark reveals where the
hunter has dug for treasure.

I see worm casts indiscriminately scattered. They
follow certain contours of the sand. I try to draw them:
loose French knots, little tubes of spaghetti chopped
off every few centimetres. There are holes too, where
something has buried itself to leave a hollow on the
sand surface.

At the point's end suddenly the waves are a flurry of
water fighting against water. As I walk round into the
wind I feel for a while I'm going nowhere. The rain
makes things harder still. The wind buffets and the
waves' noise tires.

There is such a physicalness to being here: it is all
encompassing.

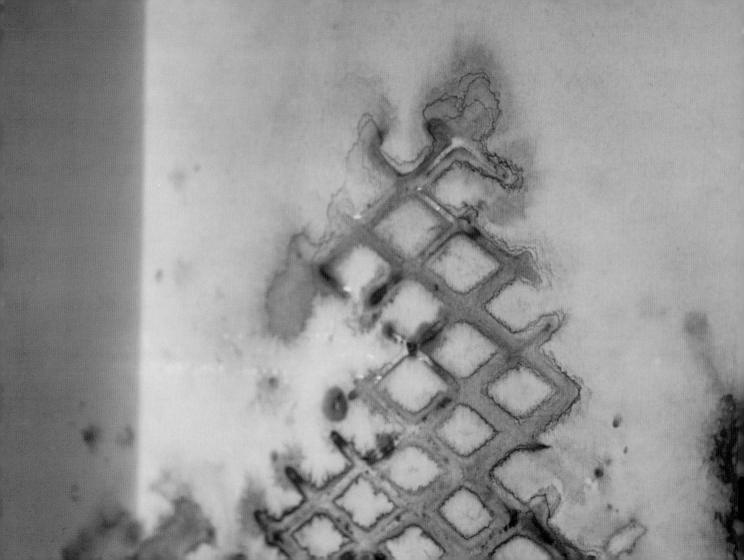

8.6.12

The road is closed by a wash-over.
There's a digger on the job
clearing the sand.

I film little sequences of ripples.
As water lies in the dips of sand,
the wind moves it in yet more ripples.

Walking south-east, I collect rusty metal.
Returning to the digger I find the road clear.

By the lighthouse I inspect the fabric bundle
left on a groyne bolt – it is still there!

9.6.12

walking

thinking

looking

collecting

listening

wondering and wandering

exploring

wind

rain

waves

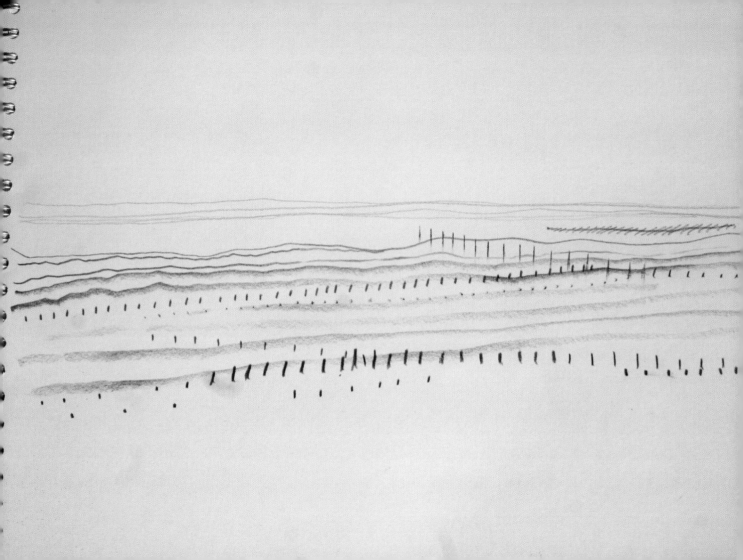

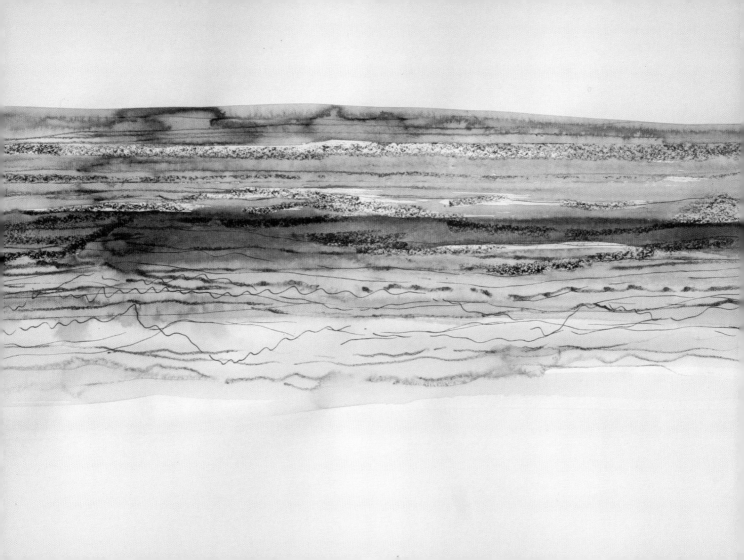

9.6.12

There is a lushness to the plant life here that wasn't
present last time I came. It is enriched when the sun shines.

The glaucous marram grass and sea buckthorn mingle with
greener greens of bramble, elder and rose. There are flowers:
white with lime green and dancing heads of lemon yellow.

Look closely and there are tiny pink flowers and bright yellow
bird's-foot trefoil. Look even closer and there are caterpillars;
not just the brown tailed moth larvae that are so abundant here
but others with spectacular hairs.

A ladybird larva hides on a leaf; an adult crosses a blade
of grass a bit further along.

On the steep path through the dunes to the beach a beetle
swims in the almost liquid sand. Some kind of woodlouse
struggles too, one I've never seen before.

29.6.12

Bright sunshine and animated clouds,
there's a keen wind from the south. It's
high tide. In the sun the water is muddy
brown then bright turquoise set before a
band of deep blue that stretches out to
the horizon. White horses in the wind.
Clouds' shadows race across the water,
rapidly changing tone and colour.

At the point sea meets river, water
fights water – the waves don't know
quite which way to go. I sense the
sheer quantity of water passing.
Massive. Powerful.

There is a clear view across the water
to Grimsby and Cleethorpes – so much
detail I've never seen before.

Swifts fly out over the point. Are they
going somewhere or just feeding?

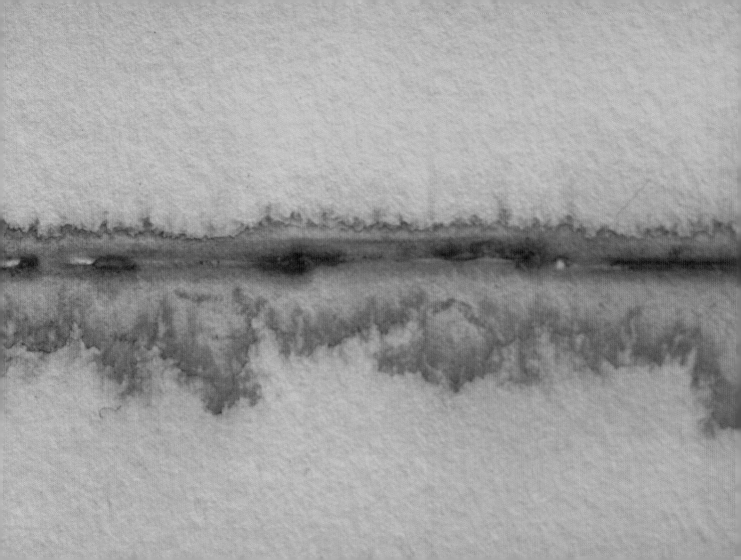

30.6.12

On the beach I undo the fabric wrapped
on the groynes. There is a certain
ceremony to this unwrapping, rich in
anticipation of what marks might be
contained within.

Submerged more often and for longer,
those wrappings further down the beach
have become part of the place: bits
of seaweed attached, holes and worn
edges, darker marks within. Those
nearer the top of the beach remain
white in places but streaked with orange
marks.

Drying on the rail in the lamp room gives
an idea of how this hanging piece might
look. Its creases catch the light. They
hold the reflective quality of water and
ripples of sand.

30.6.12

This linen cloth joins together a cascade of
marked and dyed fabric pieces. Approximately
an 8 or 10 metre drop, it is long enough to hang
in the tall room half way up the lighthouse.
I wanted the cloth to take on something of
the place itself: to get salty and sandy; to
experience the place in a way that only fabric
that had spent time wrapped and submerged by
the tides could.

I laid it out on the beach and allowed it to get
wet in the waves. The water pushed it about.
Slowly it took on the shape of the waves'
leading edge, a curved line left wet by the
movement of sand and debris.

Though dwarfed by the scale of the beach, the
length of this long and seemingly large piece
of fabric seemed right in proportion to its width:
as though a fractal reflection of this drawn out
fragment of land on which it lies.

14.7.12

Painting today from the lighthouse. I work my way round the building, using different windows and levels for their view. My aim is to collect colours, to pin down the changes in the light and the tones in the sea, the sky, the horizon. It is different every day, every hour, every minute!

The views are good, the air clear. The sea is calm. The sky is calm. There is little wind. The clouds are high and textured. The horizon switches frequently between light over dark to dark over light. The intensity of difference in tones changes constantly: sometimes a bright patch and the water glitters with reflected light; sometimes a dense mass, spreading a uniform tone. In some directions there are hints of colour; greens and chocolate browns marking zones of the water. I often see a line at the mouth of the estuary where muddy water meets clearer water. There is no mix - they remain separate.

23.7.12

(Bainside Studio, Farfield Mill, Cumbria)

Today I'm piecing together *Spurn Cloth #1*. Some larger pieces, some small, with a few very narrow strips to accentuate the horizon's dividing line: it's a patchwork of rust-dyed silk.

The all-important creases have that light-reflective quality found in water and wet sand. My stitches help to fix these in place and add further reflective qualities of their own. In placing these stitches I am responding to the marks on the silk. I use those boundaries of colour already there whilst thinking continually about how beach material, both natural and man-made, is sorted and arranged by water.

Progress is slow but steady. When people visit the studio I welcome short breaks to chat to them. The very scale of what I'm doing surprises most visitors. I'm fairly daunted by it too, but I will persevere, as it seems so right for the space it will be seen in.

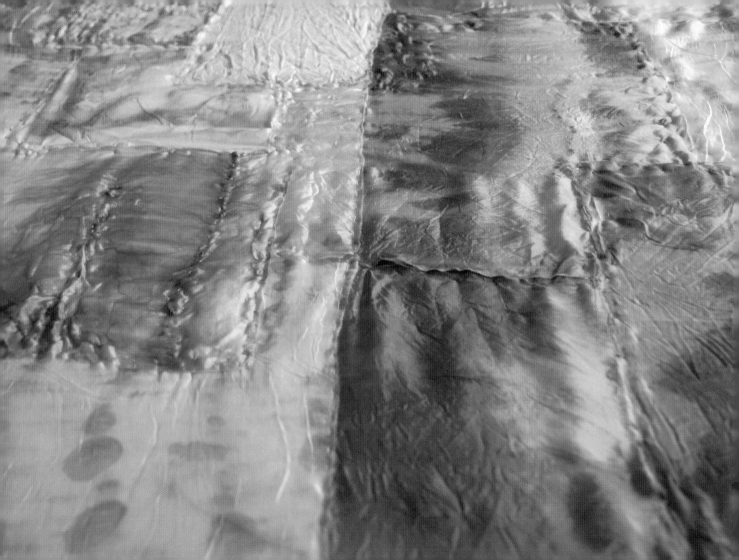

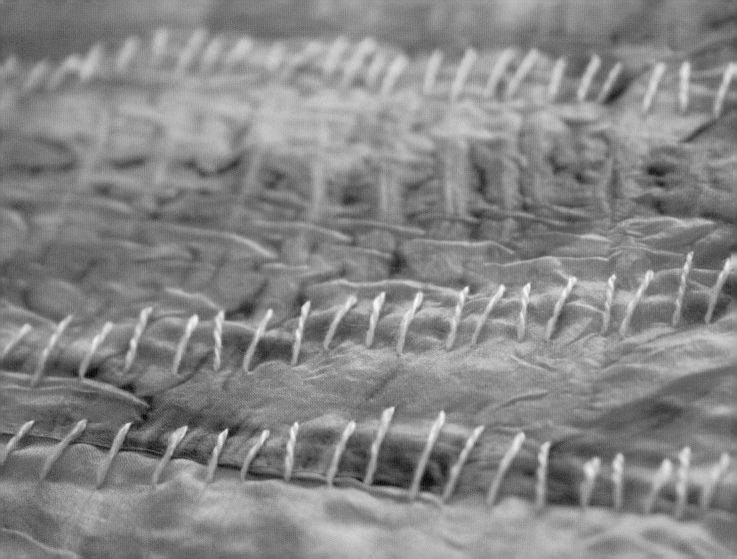

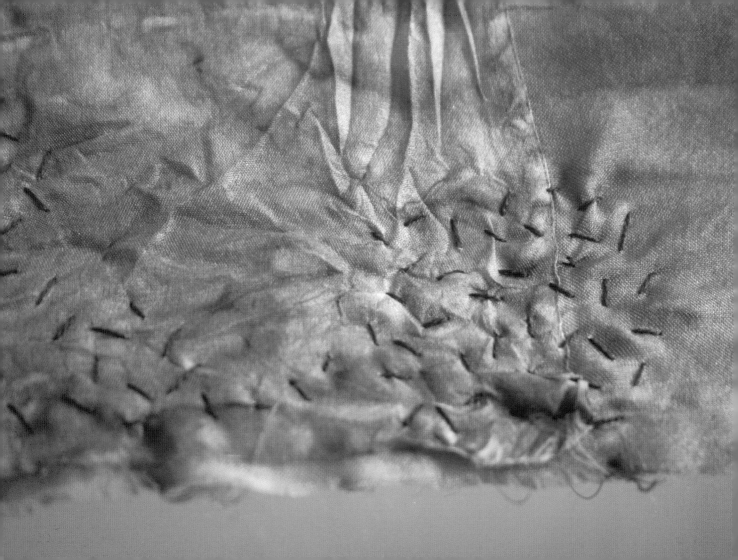

26.7.12

I started constructing *Spurn Cloth #2* today. I'm laying the whole cloth out along the floor of the studio and playing about with its separate strips until their ordering and position looks right.

It is good to see how all the textures and patterns I've been collecting on these pieces of linen will work together and how they relate to *Cloth #1*.

In *Cloth #2* I've concentrated on creating a fall of fabric made up of bands of texture. I'm using a sewing machine for this assemblage of linen pieces so joining all its strips together will be a quicker and less arduous process. The completed cloth will hang in a very tall space in the lighthouse.

23.8.12

marks made by found items
printed marks
texture
line
horizon
embossed marks,
like impressions in wet sand
impressions of objects
a moment captured
colour taken from an object to fabric or paper
marks that are ambiguous, suggestive
embodiment of marks on the beach
marks on the landscape
captured on cloth
paper as cloth
cloth and paper

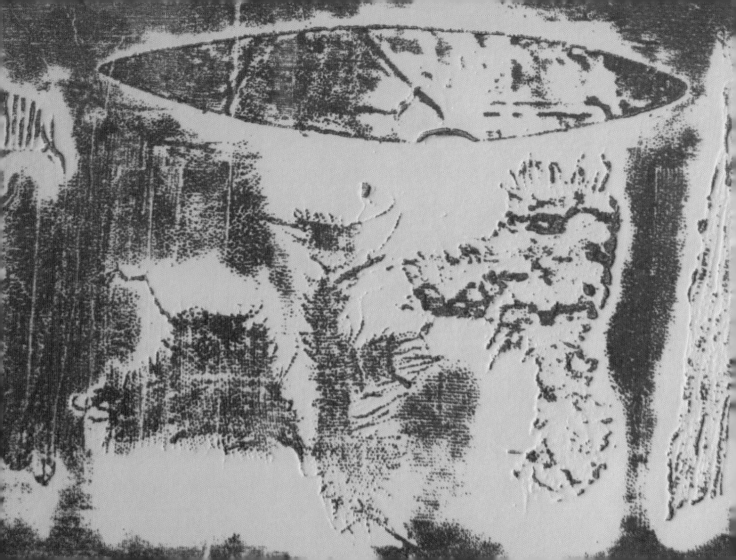

Acknowledgements

Spurn Point Artist in Residence 2012 was hosted and supported by Yorkshire Wildlife Trust. The project was supported by the National Lottery through Arts Council England. The residency exhibition in September 2012 was supported by EYEvents.

Particular thanks go to Andrew Gibson, Yorkshire Wildlife Trust, Spurn Bird Observatory, Farfield Mill, Nigel Morgan, Jilly Edwards, Ruth Brown, Sue and Andrew Wells, Jonathan and Jane Fox for their support, advice and encouragement.